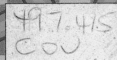

SECRETS *in* STONE

ALL ABOUT MAYA HIEROGLYPHS

BY LAURIE COULTER
ILLUSTRATIONS BY SARAH JANE ENGLISH

Historical consultation by
Dr. Elizabeth Graham and Simon Martin

A SCHOLASTIC/
MADISON PRESS BOOK

Each year thousands of visitors explore the incredible Maya archaeological sites in Mexico and Central America. They climb the steps of temples and pyramids and gaze in amazement at the cities built by this mysterious civilization. Less than two centuries ago, these ruins lay hidden in the jungle, waiting to be discovered…

LOST CITIES IN THE JUNGLE

In 1839, two explorers set out on an expedition into the jungles of Central America. The rainy season had begun, and the trail ahead of them looked like a muddy stream flowing through the dense undergrowth. It was slippery and choked with rocks and giant roots. Six days later, their local guides led the two tired, mosquito-bitten men into a village.

"Are there any ruins near here?" they asked a villager.

"Yes," he said. "Follow me."

John Lloyd Stephens, an American lawyer and travel writer, and English artist Frederick Catherwood were about to find out if the stories they had heard about Central America's lost cities were true. The villager took the excited explorers along a little-used path. At its end, he pointed across a river to what looked like an old stone wall. It soared five stories into the air!

John Lloyd Stephens.

Just inside the ruins of Copán, a huge stone head stared at the men, daring them to go any farther. Snakelike vines covered buildings. Crumbling pyramids rose through the trees. And strange carved symbols, which looked a bit like Egyptian hieroglyphs, decorated stone monuments. The only sound was the rustle of hundreds of spider monkeys in the treetops. They followed Stephens and Catherwood like ghosts through the silent city.

At the ruins of Copán, the explorers found the back of this monument, called a stela (left), covered with hieroglyphs (right). Catherwood spent many hours copying these mysterious signs into his notebooks.

In Tulum, Mexico, Catherwood drew Stephens and himself (top left and right) measuring an ancient Maya building.

THIS WAS ONE OF THE HIEROGLYPHS CATHERWOOD COPIED. YEARS LATER, RESEARCHERS THOUGHT THIS "GLYPH" WAS THE NAME OF THE MAN OR GOD ON THE FRONT OF THE STELA. THEY NICKNAMED HIM 18-RABBIT.

ANCIENT MATH

The head on the left side of the glyph looks like a rabbit wearing a crown. See page 41 to find out what the "crown" really is.

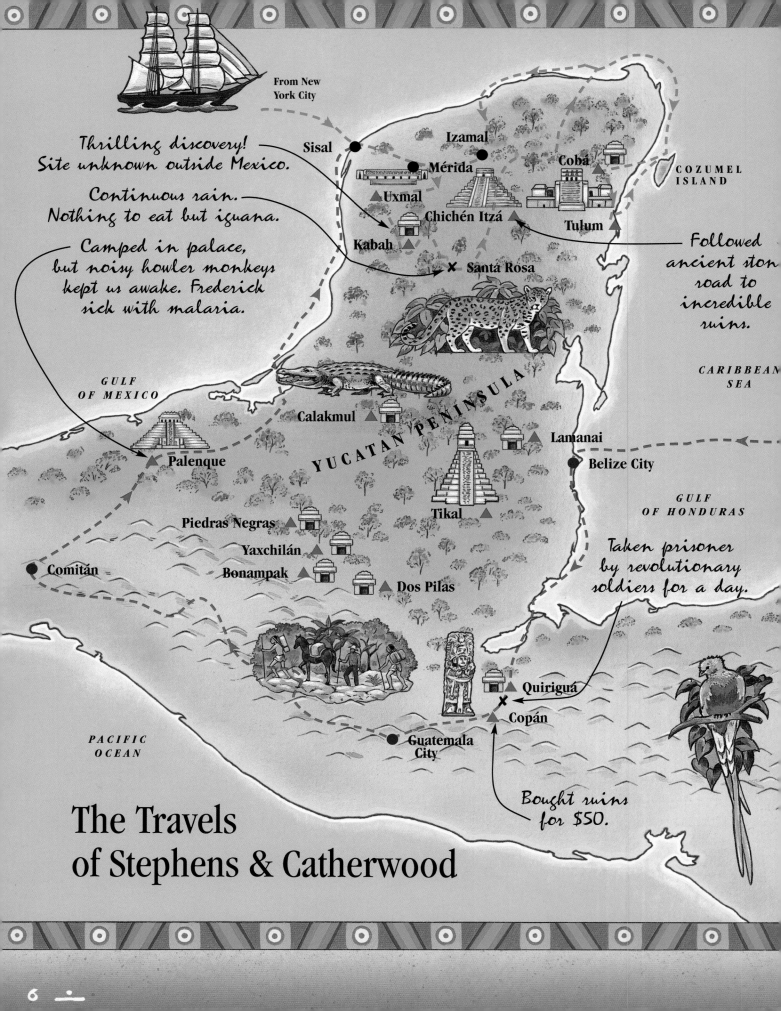

From New York City

Thrilling discovery! — Site unknown outside Mexico.

Continuous rain. — Nothing to eat but iguana.

Camped in palace, but noisy howler monkeys kept us awake. Frederick sick with malaria.

Followed ancient stone road to incredible ruins.

Taken prisoner by revolutionary soldiers for a day.

Bought ruins for $50.

Sisal

Izamal

Mérida

Cobá

COZUMEL ISLAND

Uxmal

Chichén Itzá

Tulum

Kabah

Santa Rosa

GULF OF MEXICO

CARIBBEAN SEA

Calakmul

Lamanai

Palenque

Belize City

YUCATAN PENINSULA

GULF OF HONDURAS

Tikal

Piedras Negras

Yaxchilán

Bonampak

Dos Pilas

Comitán

Quiriguá

Copán

PACIFIC OCEAN

Guatemala City

The Travels of Stephens & Catherwood

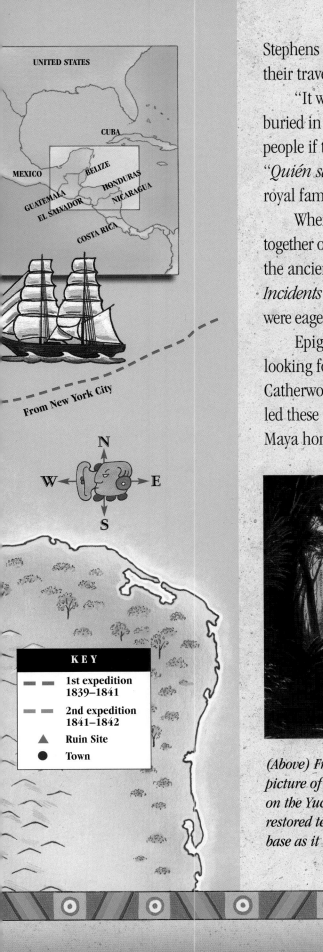

UNITED STATES

CUBA

MEXICO   BELIZE

GUATEMALA   HONDURAS

EL SALVADOR   NICARAGUA

COSTA RICA

From New York City

N

W   E

S

KEY

- - - 1st expedition
1839–1841

- - - 2nd expedition
1841–1842

▲ Ruin Site

● Town

Stephens and Catherwood visited forty-three other ancient cities on their travels through the Maya world.

"It was very mysterious," Stephens said. Each ghost city "lay buried in forests, ruined ... without a name." He asked the local people if they knew who had built the cities. But they just shrugged, "*Quién sabe?*" — "Who knows?" The names of the cities and their royal families had been forgotten long ago.

When the two explorers returned home in 1842, they worked together on a book about their remarkable journeys. Unlike the Romans, the ancient Maya had never been studied before. But after reading *Incidents of Travel in Central America*, scholars and archaeologists were eager to find out more about this unknown civilization.

Epigraphers — people who decipher ancient writing — began looking for ways to unlock the secret meanings of the hieroglyphs in Catherwood's pictures. Their search for clues to the hieroglyphic code led these "codebreakers" back in time to the Spanish Conquest of the Maya homeland in the 1500s.

(Above) Frederick Catherwood drew this picture of the main temple at Chichén Itzá on the Yucatán Peninsula. (Right) The restored temple with its pyramid base as it looks today.

THE AMAZING MAYA

Maya kings once ruled their city states from magnificent capitals with populations of up to 100,000 people and massive temples soaring ten stories into the air. By the time the Spaniards arrived, many of the larger city states of the Maya civilization's golden era — from A.D. 250 to 900 — had lain in ruins for six centuries. Many of the ancient Maya's extraordinary achievements lay hidden, too, under a sea of trees.

● Maya architects and engineers built incredible temples, palaces, houses, reservoirs, and harbors — all without metal tools.

(Above) *The Maya built more than a hundred cities with towering temples and painted palaces. This is what Palenque might have looked like at its height. The Maya also created intricate clay figurines (opposite) and bowls (below).*

● The Maya invented their own writing system. Very few other ancient civilizations did this. Most borrowed from the scripts that already existed.

● The Maya came up with the idea of zero (left), an achievement shared only by the ancient civilization of northern India and Pakistan.

● Until the telescope was used to study the stars in the early 1600s, the Maya's calendars were more accurate than the calendars of any other civilization in the world.

● The Maya created some of the world's most beautiful paintings, sculpture, and pottery.

● They were the first people to make rubber balls, an invention that eventually influenced games all over the world.

THE FIRST CLUES

The Maya, like their Aztec neighbors in Mexico, found it very difficult to win a battle against the Spanish invaders. Their bows and arrows and stone-tipped wooden spears were no match for the enemy's steel swords and guns. And as Tekun Uman and his men discovered, the Spaniards also possessed a secret weapon.

During one fierce battle, the Maya commander managed to kill the Spanish army's enormous captain with a single blow of his club. Seconds later, he watched in amazement as the dead warrior split in two. One half lay on the ground, but the other half stood up and ran towards him, his sword raised high.

Tekun Uman had never seen a horse before. He thought the animal and its rider were a single living thing. His mistake cost him his life.

Once the Maya learned about horses and the European way of fighting, they were able to defend their lands for a while. But by 1549, when a priest called Diego de Landa arrived on the Yucatán Peninsula, the Spaniards had ruled over the Maya for several years. During that time, European missionaries taught the Maya about Christianity. To make sure everyone went to church, they destroyed paintings, books, and statues that would remind the people of their own gods.

One of the last Maya lords fled with his followers to a remote village. When Landa heard that these villagers still followed the old ways, he swooped down upon them in a rage. "Burn all the books," Landa ordered the soldiers who had come with him. "They contain nothing but superstitions and falsehoods of the devil."

Three hundred years later, the codebreakers cursed Landa. The books he burned might have helped them break the Maya hieroglyphic code. Then they wondered, had any of the books survived the Spanish Conquest?

The hunt was on!

A Maya queen helps her husband prepare for battle.

THE "BIG HAMBURGER" HIEROGLYPH FOR "BOOK" LOOKS LIKE SHEETS OF PAPER FOLDED BETWEEN JAGUAR-HIDE COVERS.

MAKE-YOUR-OWN MAYA BOOKPLATES

Rub the "book" glyph and your initials, or those of a friend or relative, onto large self-adhesive labels to put on the inside front covers of books.

(Above) A Maya stone arrowhead. (Left) A Maya warrior. (Opposite) A book burning.

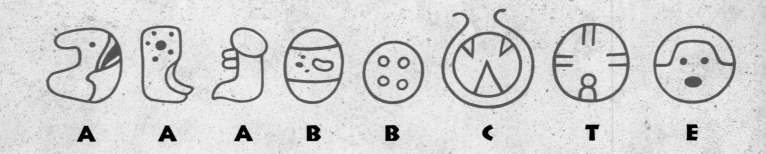

A   A   A   B   B   C   T   E

The codebreakers searched dusty library shelves throughout Europe for any Maya books written in hieroglyphs. In the 1800s, everyone who studied ancient languages wanted to be the next Jean François Champollion. In 1822, the 32-year-old French scholar became famous after he deciphered the Egyptian hieroglyphs carved on a rock found near Rosetta in Egypt.

Incredibly, the codebreakers found three "codices" — accordion-folded books made by Maya scribes. Centuries ago, Spanish soldiers had probably sent these books back to Europe as New World curiosities. They had been filed away and forgotten in libraries in Dresden, Germany; Madrid, Spain; and Paris, France.

In a Spanish library, the codebreakers also found a book written by Diego de Landa. In his book called *Relación de las Cosas de Yucatán*, the priest wrote out a Maya "alphabet" (above). Their curses turned to cheers. Finally! the codebreakers thought. Our own Rosetta Stone!

Maya scribes folded paper made from the inner bark of fig trees into a kind of book, which we call a codex.

(Above)
A noblewoman,
who may have
been a scribe,
holds a codex.

(Left)
A small section
of the 74-page
Dresden Codex.
The entire book
is more than
11 feet (3 m)
long when
spread out flat.

GLYPH SEARCH
Can you find Maya
bar and dot numbers
(see page 16) in the
Dresden Codex
(above)?

THE GLYPH
FOR "SCRIBE"
SHOWS
A SCRIBE'S
HAND
HOLDING
A PEN.

IN THE HOUSE OF THE VAMPIRE BAT

The next important discovery was made in the 1850s. Abbé Charles Brasseur de Bourbourg found a sixteenth-century copy of the *Popol Vuh*, the creation story of the Maya of Guatemala. Discovering this 9,000-line poem was like finding a Maya Bible. Nevertheless, the Maya words in the *Popol Vuh* had been written in Spanish letters, not hieroglyphs. The early codebreakers still pinned their hopes on Landa's "alphabet."

This is a story from the *Popol Vuh* about the adventures of two brothers:

Hunahpu and Xbalanque, the twin sons of the Maize God and Blood Moon, made so much noise playing ball that they upset the Lords of Death, who lived under the ball court. As punishment, the two brothers were forced to travel to the Underworld, called Xibalba. There they had to pass several death-defying tests.

After moving safely through five houses of torture, the brothers were locked inside the house of Zotz, the vampire bat. Using their magic powers, they hid that night in their blowguns. Unfortunately, Hunahpu stuck his head out in the morning to see if the day had begun, and Zotz quickly swooped down and tore it off!

The Xibalbans made Xbalanque play a ball game with them, using his brother's head as a ball. But he fooled them. When they weren't looking, he cleverly fit the head back on Hunahpu's body.

After performing many magical feats, the twins were ordered to kill themselves. They did, but immediately sprang back to life. "Perform this trick on us," the Lords of Death demanded.

"All right," Hunahpu and Xbalanque said, smiling at each other. They cut two important Lords into small pieces, then refused to bring them back to life. The remaining Lords ran away.

After conquering Xibalba, the Hero Twins rose into the sky and became the Sun and Venus. Death had been outwitted, bringing hope to all people.

THE GLYPH FOR "BAT" WAS ONE OF THE FIRST HIEROGLYPHS DECIPHERED.

(Left) An ancient vase from Guatemala shows Zotz with pictures of plucked-out eyeballs on his wings. (Opposite) The killer bat swoops down on Hunahpu.

Maya farmers sold the food they grew or the goods they made in the markets of villages, towns, and cities.

● One gourd: Split in half, gourds were used as cups, containers, and even chamberpots!

●● Two seashells: Jewelry, scribe's paint pots, and trumpets were made from shells.

●●● Three cotton blankets.

●●●● Four clay pots.

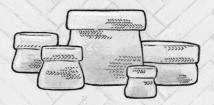

▬ Five baskets.

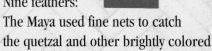

● / ▬ Six cobs of corn: Maize (corn) was the most important Maya food. They grew several kinds, from yellow to deep blue in color.

●● Seven fish.

●●● Eight chili peppers.

●●●● Nine feathers:
The Maya used fine nets to catch the quetzal and other brightly colored birds. They plucked a few feathers, then let the bird go. The feathers were used to decorate clothing, headdresses, and earrings.

Ten cakes of salt.

COUNTING AND CALENDARS

For many years, the codebreakers tried to connect this letter and that letter from Landa's alphabet with the hieroglyphs in the three Maya codices. Finally they gave up. His alphabet just didn't seem to work. But in the 1880s, a German librarian named Ernst Förstemann spent many hours studying the Dresden Codex (see page 13) and was one of the first people to work out the Maya way of counting.

They used a dot ● for one, a bar ▬ for five, and a shell ⬯ or flower ⬮ for zero. The numbers could be written ●●● horizontally or vertically. This was far simpler and more efficient than the arithmetic used by the Romans, who lived at the same time. The Romans used seven symbols for numbers — I (1), V (5), X (10), L (50), C (100), D (500), M (1,000). Even our own Arabic system uses nine symbols.

CHOCOLATE MONEY

The ancient Maya loved chocolate, which they made from roasted or ground cacao beans. Because cacao trees (top) could only be grown in tropical forests, chocolate was very valuable throughout the Maya world and beyond. For instance, the Aztecs in Mexico bought chocolate from the Maya. Chocolate was so valuable, in fact, that the Maya sometimes used the beans as money. (Archaeologists have even found counterfeit beans of clay.)

THE NUMBER OF THE UNIVERSE

Some people believe that 7 is a lucky number and 13 is unlucky. The ancient Maya believed 3 was a special number because their universe had three layers — the Overworld (the heavens), the Middleworld (the world of people), and the Underworld, or Xibalba (the place of disease and death).

At the center of the world grew a giant ceiba tree (above). The World Tree's branches supported the sky in the Overworld. Its trunk rose through the Middleworld. And its roots stretched into the Underworld beneath the earth or the sea. The Maya gods and the souls of the dead used this tree as a pathway to the three worlds.

(Above) *Bird Jaguar, a Maya king, holds up his spear as his wife looks on.*

THE "STAR WAR" GLYPH (RIGHT) APPEARS IN INSCRIPTIONS ABOUT WAR.

Like doodlers who often fill every bit of space, Maya scribes sometimes used a half-circle as a space filler between number dots.

GLYPH SEARCH — Can you find the "star war" glyph, a space filler, and the numbers 7 and 14 in the top left of this stone carving?

Once he understood Maya arithmetic, math wizard Ernst Förstemann began to figure out how these ancient people kept track of time.

The Maya, like all early peoples, believed the journeys of the stars and planets across the sky represented supernatural forces. The only way to control these forces was to be able to predict where the stars would be at any given time. So each day, their astronomers marked down the positions of the sun, moon, stars, and planets in relation to a building or a marker set in the ground. They used these records to put together calendars and almanacs.

The almanacs showed eclipses, full moons, and the appearances of certain stars. Maya kings studied them to decide when to hold important events in their kingdoms.

VENUS STAR WARS

Like today's astronomers, Maya starwatchers could predict when Venus would be visible as an evening or a morning star. Maya kings may have planned military campaigns for the days when Venus, a planet they associated with war, was visible in the western sky.

Before a "star war," the king's warriors sharpened their spears and stabbing knives. They smeared their bodies with red and black paint and put on padded cotton armor and fancy helmets. Then they followed their king to the enemy city. As the raid began, the terrifying sound of shrill whistles and conch-shell trumpets filled the air.

In a star war, a ruler proved how powerful he was by capturing a rival king (see page 32) and taking valuable goods from the defeated city as tribute.

(Left) The Maya may have used this building at Chichén Itzá as an astronomical observatory.

(Right) Tikal in Guatemala was used as the model for the rebel base in the movie Star Wars.

WHEELS OF TIME

The Maya didn't just count on their fingers. They used their toes, too! With one exception, they recorded the passing of time in multiples of 20. (We use 10 in our decimal system.) They began with a day, or *k'in*. Then they moved up to a month, or *winal* (20 k'ins), a *tun* (18 winals or 360 days), a *k'atun* (20 tuns or 7,200 days), and a *bak'tun* (20 k'atuns or 144,000 days).

| **K'IN** | **WINAL** | **TUN** | **K'ATUN** | **BAK'TUN** |

THE WHEELS OF TIME GET BIGGER AND BIGGER

Our own Gregorian calendar is a cycle or wheel of time beginning on January 1 and ending on December 31. Then we begin again with a new cycle. We try to make our "year" equal the time it takes for the earth to revolve around the sun — about 365 days. Our "months" are based on the time it takes the moon to complete its phases from new moon to full moon.

The Maya also had two main wheels of time — a 260-day sacred calendar (the *tzolk'in*) for planning religious rituals and a 365-day solar calendar (the *haab*).

THE CALENDAR ROUND

The sacred calendar and the solar calendar fit together like the gears on a bicycle chain to give a combined date, one from each calendar — for example, 1 Akbal, 1 Pop (see illustration on opposite page). This is similar to a date in our calendar such as Saturday, January 1. Saturday is Day 7 of the week. January 1 is Day 1 of the first month of the year.

Once every 18,980 days (365 x 52 days), the first day of each calendar reappears and the cycle begins again. This 52-year cycle is called the Calendar Round.

(Left) A toy jaguar.

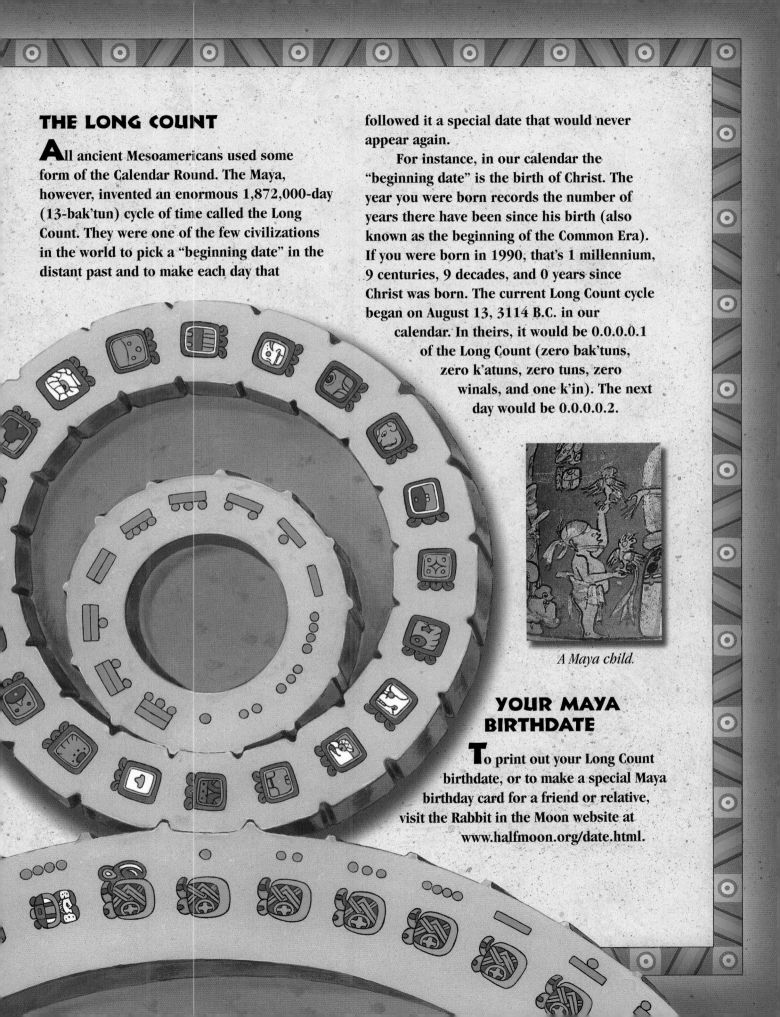

THE LONG COUNT

All ancient Mesoamericans used some form of the Calendar Round. The Maya, however, invented an enormous 1,872,000-day (13-bak'tun) cycle of time called the Long Count. They were one of the few civilizations in the world to pick a "beginning date" in the distant past and to make each day that followed it a special date that would never appear again.

For instance, in our calendar the "beginning date" is the birth of Christ. The year you were born records the number of years there have been since his birth (also known as the beginning of the Common Era). If you were born in 1990, that's 1 millennium, 9 centuries, 9 decades, and 0 years since Christ was born. The current Long Count cycle began on August 13, 3114 B.C. in our calendar. In theirs, it would be 0.0.0.0.1 of the Long Count (zero bak'tuns, zero k'atuns, zero tuns, zero winals, and one k'in). The next day would be 0.0.0.0.2.

A Maya child.

YOUR MAYA BIRTHDATE

To print out your Long Count birthdate, or to make a special Maya birthday card for a friend or relative, visit the Rabbit in the Moon website at www.halfmoon.org/date.html.

THE DAY THE WORLD ENDS

The early codebreakers stared at the same old glyphs in the same old books. They were getting nowhere. Then along came English explorer Alfred Percival Maudslay.

In the 1880s, after reading Stephens and Catherwood's book, Maudslay hiked into the rainforests of Central America to photograph the Maya ruins for the first time. Lugging a huge camera along the jungle paths, he took pictures of the buildings, art, and hieroglyphs he saw. He also made plaster molds of the intricate monuments.

On his return from his seventh and final trip, Maudslay hired an artist, Annie Hunter. He asked her to make drawings of the plaster casts. In 1889, he began publishing her pictures and his photographs in a series of books. The thankful codebreakers now had big, accurately drawn chunks of Maya writing to decipher.

They studied the hieroglyphs in Maudslay's books and figured out what the Maya dates were in our calendar system. For example, on December 23, 2012, the current Long Count cycle ends.

In A.D. 600 to 800, a scribe included himself in the center of this vase painting (opposite). A thousand years later, Alfred Maudslay (below) arrived in Central America to photograph what remained of the scribe's world. (Bottom) A Maya child sits beside a stela.

GLYPH SEARCH

 Can you find the ahaw month sign in the vase painting on page 22?

DECEMBER 23, 2012

Did the ancient Maya believe the world would come to an end on this milestone date? Some people think they did. But others point out that one king predicted that the day he was crowned would still be celebrated at the end of an 8,000-year cycle. That year would be 4772 in our calendar — nearly 2,800 years after the so-called end of the world!

This Long Count date for December 23, 2012, reads (from left to right) 13 bak'tuns, zero k'atuns, zero tuns, zero winals and zero k'ins, 4 ahaw, 3 kankin, Lord of the Night 9.

MAUDSLAY NOTICED THAT A BIG HIEROGLYPH BEGINS MOST PIECES OF MAYA WRITING. HE CALLED THIS EASY-TO-SPOT "HERE'S THE BEGINNING" SIGN THE INTRODUCTORY GLYPH.

BREAKING THE CODE

For generations, the people of the Yucatán Peninsula chewed gum made from the sap, called *chicle,* of the sapodilla tree. In other parts of the world, people made gum from sweetened paraffin wax — just like the bright red wax lips sold in candy stores today.

An American candymaker brought out a "Snapping and Stretching" gum made from chicle in the 1890s. Chiclets soon became the best-selling brand. Gum manufacturers had to look for new groves of sapodilla trees just to keep up with the demand. In their search, chicle-hunters cleared trails through the Maya lowland jungles. These trails led to the discovery of some very important Maya archaeological sites, including Yaxchilán, Seibal, and Piedras Negras.

The codebreakers pored over photographs of hieroglyphs from these newly found cities. More years went by. Many of the frustrated codebreakers said, "Forget it! Maya glyphs aren't like Egyptian hieroglyphs. They *cannot* be read. They're just holy signs, dates, and the names of gods and goddesses."

But they were wrong. Two codebreakers suddenly found some exciting patterns. If you look at the family trees of today's kings and queens, you will see a pattern, too. The same words — *born, crowned, died* — appear after each name. These words are followed by a date. This was the type of pattern the codebreakers began to see.

HEINRICH'S EMBLEM GLYPHS

In 1958, Heinrich Berlin, a German businessman living in Mexico, found the same interesting small signs on hieroglyphs from several different Maya sites. They looked like two squashed circles and drops of water. The main part of the glyph changed from place to place.

Just as a flag is an emblem or symbol of a country, Berlin thought these special glyphs might be emblems of the cities in which they appeared.

A year later, an American art historian named Tatiana Proskouriakoff found a strange pattern of dates. She had made a chart of all the dates appearing on the stelae at the Maya site of

MAKE-YOUR-OWN EMBLEM GLYPH

Use the squashed circles on the "lord" glyph. Add your initials and the glyph for "bedroom" and place it on the door of your room. For Mother's or Father's Day, you could decorate a homemade card with a "lord or lady of the house" emblem glyph. Use the "lord" or "lady" glyphs and the "house" glyph.

THE EMBLEM GLYPH FOR YAXCHILAN.

DIVINE KINGS

A Maya king was known as a *k'uhul ahaw* or "holy lord." During the golden era, there may have been as many as sixty kings. Each one ruled over a kingdom of about 40,000 people, although Tikal may have had as many as 100,000!

Some kingdoms became much more powerful than others and organized military alliances. The two most important groups were centered on Tikal and Calakmul. Local rulers paid tribute to the high kings of these two superpowers.

All of the Maya kings were high priests as well as rulers. The king played the central role in the many sacred feasts, rituals, and festivals held throughout the year.

This jade death mask was found in a king's tomb in Palenque (see page 26).

Piedras Negras. Over and over again, the number of years between the first and last dates on each monument was no longer than 56 to 64 years — the lifetime of an average person.

She believed the stone faces of real kings and queens — not gods and goddesses — stared out from the stelae. Maybe the hieroglyphs told about their lives. Maybe the glyphs could be read after all!

(LEFT) TATIANA PROSKOURIAKOFF DECIDED THAT THE "UPTURNED FROG GLYPH" (RIGHT) MEANT "BIRTH" AND THE "TOOTHACHE GLYPH" (FAR RIGHT) MEANT "ACCESSION TO THE THRONE."

A TEMPLE'S HIDDEN TREASURE

His flashlight's beam picked out six human skeletons. The five men and one woman had been sacrificed. Their bodies had been placed together at the sealed entrance to the king's tomb. It had taken Mexican archaeologist Alberto Ruz Lhuillier and his team two years of hard work to reach this door of the dead. Behind it, they would make one of the most exciting archaeological finds of the twentieth century.

In 1949, Dr. Ruz had been working in a room at the top of Palenque's Temple of the Inscriptions. Its floor looked like a jigsaw puzzle of stone slabs. Just by chance, he noticed fingerholes, like those on a trapdoor, carved into one of the slabs. When he lifted up the slab, he discovered a secret stairway!

Cut stones and rubble completely blocked the stairs. But Ruz knew that something important must lie at the bottom. He and his archaeological team began digging. Three years and 67 steps later, they reached the bottom.

The men pulled and shoved at the triangular slab of rock sealing the entry to the tomb. Once inside, they walked down five steps into a damp, narrow room. In its center stood a coffin made from an immense block of stone. Ruz gasped when he saw it. The 12-foot (4-m) long limestone lid of the sarcophagus was carved with some of the most beautiful artwork and hieroglyphs he had ever seen.

The archaeological team carefully jacked up the five-ton lid. Inside they found the skeleton of a king surrounded by precious jade jewelry. A hollow stone tube ran from inside the tomb all the way up the stairs. Thirteen centuries ago, this spirit tube had connected the dead ruler with the world of the living above.

In 1952, nobody even knew the name of this once-great Maya king. Then just twenty-one years later, a small group of codebreakers figured out the king's name — and broke the Maya code at the same time.

"WE'VE GOT IT!"

In December 1973, Australian Peter Mathews and Americans Linda Schele and Michael Coe met at a conference on the ancient Maya in Palenque.

"Should Peter and I see if we can find more rulers?" asked Linda during a meeting on hieroglyphs.

THE NAME GLYPH OF THE KING BURIED IN THE TEMPLE OF THE INSCRIPTIONS LOOKS LIKE THE LITTLE SHIELD MAYA WARRIORS STRAPPED ON THEIR WRISTS, SO EPIGRAPHERS NICKNAMED HIM "SHIELD."

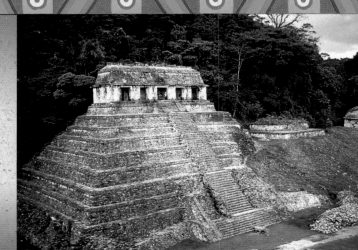

"Sure, why not?" replied Michael Coe, who was leading the meeting. "Linda, you know every stone in Palenque, and Peter knows every glyph. Why don't the two of you see if you can put together a history of Palenque's rulers? No one has tried that yet."

As Peter and Linda settled down at a table to look at pages of hieroglyphs, Floyd Lounsbury joined them. The Yale University professor was a linguist — a person who studies spoken languages.

Back in the 1950s, a Russian epigrapher suggested that some of the Maya glyphs stood for sounds like "ba" or "be" rather than letters. Sadly, only Canadian scholar David Kelley and a few other people listened to Yuri Knorosov then. But by the time of the Palenque meeting, many codebreakers believed the ancient Maya scribes spoke and wrote a version of today's Cholan or Yucatec languages.

Floyd understood how a sentence

(Opposite) The Temple of the Inscriptions at Palenque.
(Above) The image on the sarcophagus lid shows the king falling into the Underworld. (Right) Linda Schele studies a stela.

SECRET NAME CODE
To make up secret names, choose glyphs from the GlyphMaster for yourself and the people you know.

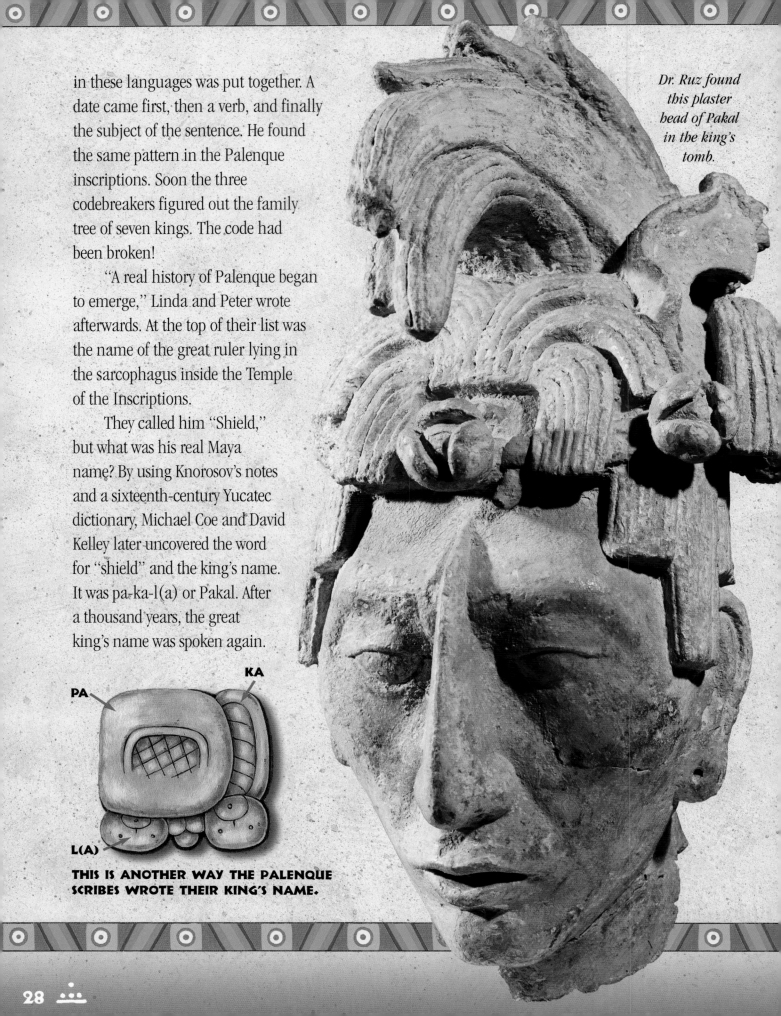

in these languages was put together. A date came first, then a verb, and finally the subject of the sentence. He found the same pattern in the Palenque inscriptions. Soon the three codebreakers figured out the family tree of seven kings. The code had been broken!

"A real history of Palenque began to emerge," Linda and Peter wrote afterwards. At the top of their list was the name of the great ruler lying in the sarcophagus inside the Temple of the Inscriptions.

They called him "Shield," but what was his real Maya name? By using Knorosov's notes and a sixteenth-century Yucatec dictionary, Michael Coe and David Kelley later uncovered the word for "shield" and the king's name. It was pa-ka-l(a) or Pakal. After a thousand years, the great king's name was spoken again.

Dr. Ruz found this plaster head of Pakal in the king's tomb.

PA

KA

L(A)

THIS IS ANOTHER WAY THE PALENQUE SCRIBES WROTE THEIR KING'S NAME.

MAYA WORD SEARCH

BLOCKS AND BLOCKHEADS

Looking at Maya hieroglyphs is like looking at a plate of spaghetti, someone once said. How do you make any sense of all those heads, swirls, and squiggles? Because you probably don't speak Yucatec or Cholan, you won't be able to "read" the Maya writing system. But you can learn how it works and what some of the glyphs mean.

A Maya scribe put signs together to make a hieroglyph. He drew them in a glyph block. This block held a main sign by itself or a main sign with several smaller signs around it. Glyph blocks were stacked together in pairs to make the Maya version of a sentence.

Like us, the Maya read from left to right. They read across one pair of glyph blocks, then skipped down to the next pair, and so on to the bottom of the column. Then they began at the top of the next column.

IT'S A JAGUAR!

Sometimes the Maya used one glyph to stand for a whole word. These logographs, or word signs, are like our symbols for "washroom" or "no smoking." The picture says it all.

Animal logographs were some of the first glyphs deciphered. The top one stands for *balam*, the Yucatec word for "jaguar." (Like the lion in other cultures, the powerful jaguar was a symbol of royalty.)

ARE YOU SURE IT'S NOT AN OCELOT?

We sometimes use the symbol plus the words "No Smoking" to make a clearer message. If the scribes wanted to make sure their readers didn't think a "jaguar" glyph stood for "ocelot," another spotted cat, they drew it this way (middle). Since the word for "ocelot" didn't begin with the sound "ba," they drew the syllable sign for "ba" in front of the jaguar head.

MAKING ABSOLUTELY SURE

We sometimes write NO SMOKING! and drop the symbol. The scribes could do this, too. They used "ba," "la," and "ma" from their syllabary (see page 44) to spell *balam(a)* (bottom). The final vowel wasn't pronounced.

Codebreakers number the columns like this.

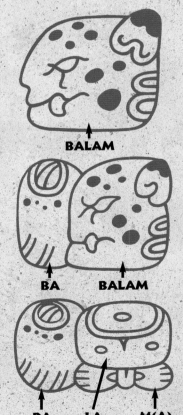

BALAM

BA   BALAM

BA   LA   M(A)

VULTURE   **LORD**

IS THAT A VULTURE OR A KING?

One glyph could also mean different things — just like our homonyms that sound the same but mean something different ("aunt," "ant"). This vulture's head glyph stands for the black-headed vulture, *tahol*, which means "excrement head"! Or it could mean *ta* — the first part of *tahol* — "to," "on," "with," or "from." The same bird with a headband means *ahaw*, "lord."

FIND THE PATTERN

The codebreakers found a pattern in most Maya writing. The calendar date glyphs were followed by a glyph that told what happened on that date. These glyphs were followed by the name and titles of the important person the scribe was writing about.

DATE GLYPHS

In addition to the calendar date (see page 23), you might also see the "it was completed" sign (1). The second sign (2) told when a period of time had ended. This may have been a time of celebration; for example, the celebration of a king's accession to the throne (3).

(1)
IT WAS COMPLETED   **(2)**
THE 1ST K'ATUN   **(3)**
IN THE REIGN

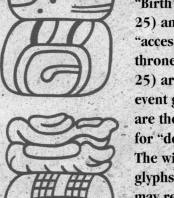

EVENT GLYPHS

"Birth" (page 25) and "accession to the throne" (page 25) are common event glyphs, as are the glyphs for "death." The wing-shell glyphs for death may refer to the flight of the spirit from the body.

DEATH

NAME AND TITLE GLYPHS

The glyph on the right and the first one below stand for *ahaw* ("lord"). The first one appears in emblem glyphs (see page 24). Today codebreakers know emblem glyphs mean "lord of such-and-such a kingdom." The next glyph stands for *ixik* ("lady"). And the last glyph is a title for young princes in line for the throne. If Prince William of England had lived in ancient Maya times, this title would have appeared before his name.

LORD

LORD   **LADY**   **PRINCE**

FAMILY GLYPHS

CHILD OF (FATHER'S NAME) **CHILD OF (MOTHER'S NAME)** **THE LOVED ONE** **YOUNGER BROTHER**

A noblewoman kneels before a king in this vase painting from A.D. 600 to 800.

"MAKE IT FANCY," THE KING COMMANDED

People have always had fun playing with letters, signs, and punctuation in their writing. We use keyboard  faces (:–) "happy" ; :-# "my lips are sealed") to stand for certain words in e-mail messages. Or we write the same word in different ways: &, and, or AND, for example.

The Maya liked to do this, too. At Copán, the scribes seemed to have had a contest to see how many different ways they could write King Yax Pasah's name and titles. The codebreakers took years to unscramble them!

KING YAX PASAH

NORTH   **NORTH**   **NORTH**

Each Maya scribe had his own way of writing the glyphs, just as you have your own way of writing the letters of our alphabet. Sometimes a king asked his scribes to use a style of writing that he liked best. Here's the glyph for "north" written by three different scribes.

THE SEARCH CONTINUES...

ADVENTURES OF A TEENAGE CODEBREAKER

David Stuart's family has probably visited more Maya ruins than any other family in the world. His father was *National Geographic* magazine's archaeological editor. And his parents once wrote a book together called *The Mysterious Maya*.

During the summers of 1974 and 1975, the Stuarts lived in a small thatch-roofed house at the Coba archaeological site in Mexico. While his parents made maps of the ancient city, ten-year-old David played with the local Maya children.

WHILE DAVID STUART (LEFT) WAS STILL A TEENAGER, HE DECIPHERED THE "COUNT-OF-CAPTIVES" GLYPH. SCRIBES OFTEN PUT THIS SIGN BETWEEN THE GLYPH FOR THEIR KING'S NAME AND THE ONE FOR HIS CITY. THE NUMBER OF MEN A KING HAD CAPTURED IN BATTLE SHOWED HOW POWERFUL HE WAS.

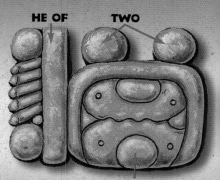

HE OF   TWO

CAPTIVES

One day the project's workers uncovered two new stelae. As George Stuart drew pictures of the beautifully carved monuments, his son made his own drawings and in the weeks that followed began learning about Maya hieroglyphs.

David turned out to be a glyph wizard. When he was only fifteen, he served as the epigrapher for a *National Geographic* expedition. The group spent several days exploring caves in Guatemala. Just three years later, David's picture appeared in all the newspapers. He had been awarded a MacArthur Fellowship of U.S. $128,000 (worth $500,000 today!) to help him continue his Maya hieroglyphic work. He was the youngest person ever to be given this special academic honor.

David Stuart's interest in glyphs never waned, and today he is Associate Director of the Corpus of Maya Hieroglyphs at Harvard University's Peabody Museum.

BLOODLETTING AND SACRIFICE

The ancient Maya believed humans and gods depended upon one another for survival. Gods gave people the gifts of life, good health, and food. In return, humans gave the gods offerings, particularly the precious gift of human blood. Maya kings and queens drew blood from their ears, lips, and tongues with a sharp object. The blood dripped onto paper strips held in special pottery bowls. Then the paper was set on fire. When the smoke rose up into the Overworld, it was consumed by the gods. In these personal bloodletting ceremonies, the king went into a dreamlike state so that he could enter the spirit world and ask the gods for help for his people.

The most important Maya ceremonies, such as the crowning or burial of a ruler, sometimes required human sacrifice, perhaps because this was a period of transition, when people felt afraid of the unknown. These acts of sacrifice showed the religious and political power of the king.

(Above) A king wearing a jaguar skin marches a royal captive back to his city. The captive's battle gear and ear ornament (inset) have been removed. (Right) A royal couple conduct a bloodletting ritual. He is holding a torch while she passes a thorned cord through her tongue.

THE GLYPH FOR "BLOOD-LETTER."

A WHOLE DIFFERENT BALL GAME

The codebreakers were completely baffled — yet again. They had discovered the glyph for the fast, dangerous ball game that was played throughout the Maya world. But the Maya word for the game remained a mystery.

Paintings on pottery, stone carvings, and Spanish accounts of the Aztec ball game provide the only clues to the game's rules. At Chichén Itzá, the players on each team may have tried to hit the ball through a huge stone ring hung on a wall. But at many sites, the slanted walls of the playing court suggest that the players bounced the ball off the walls like modern handball players.

THE GLYPH FOR "BALL COURT" SHOWS A CROSS-SECTION OF THE COURT WITH A BALL IN THE CENTER.

(Left) The ball court at Copán.

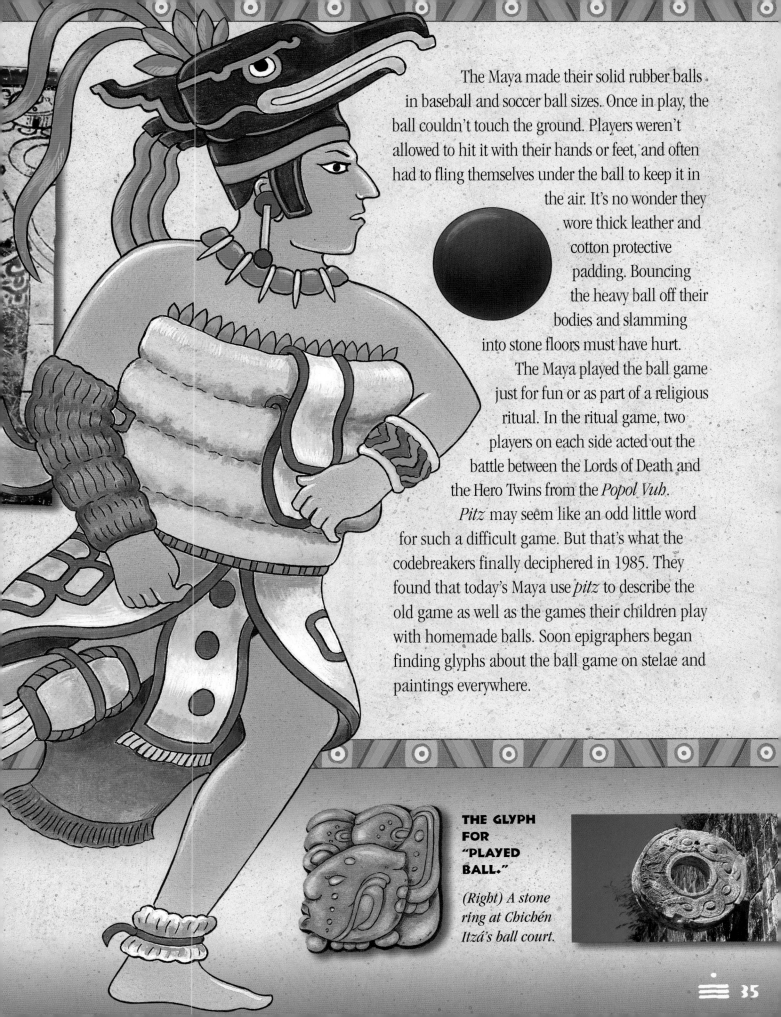

The Maya made their solid rubber balls in baseball and soccer ball sizes. Once in play, the ball couldn't touch the ground. Players weren't allowed to hit it with their hands or feet, and often had to fling themselves under the ball to keep it in the air. It's no wonder they wore thick leather and cotton protective padding. Bouncing the heavy ball off their bodies and slamming into stone floors must have hurt.

The Maya played the ball game just for fun or as part of a religious ritual. In the ritual game, two players on each side acted out the battle between the Lords of Death and the Hero Twins from the *Popol Vuh*.

Pitz may seem like an odd little word for such a difficult game. But that's what the codebreakers finally deciphered in 1985. They found that today's Maya use *pitz* to describe the old game as well as the games their children play with homemade balls. Soon epigraphers began finding glyphs about the ball game on stelae and paintings everywhere.

THE GLYPH FOR "PLAYED BALL."

(Right) A stone ring at Chichén Itzá's ball court.

MY FOAMY CHOCOLATE DRINK

Pile up cacao beans and let them ferment, then dry and roast them. Grind the cacao beans and mix with water. Add a dash of vanilla, chili, or honey. To make the drink foamy, pour the mixture from one container into another. And, voila, you have the Maya's favorite drink, *kakaw*. Chocolate was also used in sauces, such as molé sauce on cooked turkey.

The glyph on the far left of this ancient screw-top container's lid says "cacao" (chocolate). The entire inscription says, "his drinking vessel for the seasoned cacao."

Archaeologists sent the dried material inside this container to the Hershey Foods Corporation in Pennsylvania for analysis. The tests confirmed that it was very, very old chocolate.

THAT'S MINE!

The ancient Maya liked to put their names on their belongings. In the 1980s, Peter Mathews found the first example of "name-tagging" on a pair of large earrings discovered in a royal tomb in Belize. The glyph for "his" or "her" was followed by the glyph for "ear flare" (top right) and the glyphs for the owner's name. The Maya also name-tagged important rooms and buildings.

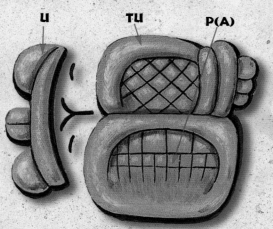

U   TU   P(A)

**THE GLYPH FOR "HIS ('U')
EAR FLARE ('TUP(A)')."**

MAYA BEAUTY TIPS

PIERCED EARS

The Maya pierced their earlobes and wore many kinds of ear ornaments. Kings and queens, for example, wore ear flares. When a ruler was defeated in battle, these ornaments were removed. In Maya art, royal captives sometimes wear strips of paper in the place of their seized ear flares (see page 32).

FANCY TEETH

And you thought braces were bad! The Maya ruling class sometimes ground one or more small holes into their tooth enamel to hold circular pieces of jade, pyrite, or other precious stones. Copal, a tree sap, may have been used to deaden the pain. They also filed the edges of their front teeth in different patterns.

The royal women in this mural from Bonampak have put on their best jade jewelry. Although they look as though they are putting on makeup, they are actually preparing to pierce their tongues in a sacred bloodletting ritual.

These ear flares look like the little trumpet flowers of the ceiba tree.

A sculpture of a Maya noble- woman and her baby, both with flattened foreheads.

PAINTED AND TATTOOED BODIES

On special occasions, the Maya painted their faces to look like the faces of gods. They also painted and tattooed their bodies.

COVER THAT NAVEL!

The Maya lord's loincloth, hip-cloth, and cape, and the Maya lady's huipil (a loose-fitting sleeveless blouse worn over a skirt) always covered the navel. The Maya may have thought showing your bellybutton was very rude.

FLATTENED FOREHEADS

The Maya nobility considered a sloping forehead attractive. Kings were often drawn in profile to show off their stylish heads. The Spaniards reported that mothers tied the heads of their newborn babies between two boards for several days. Because newborns' skulls are still soft, they would be flattened for life after this beauty treatment. But Maya burial sites, especially from the golden era, show that this practice was not followed by everyone.

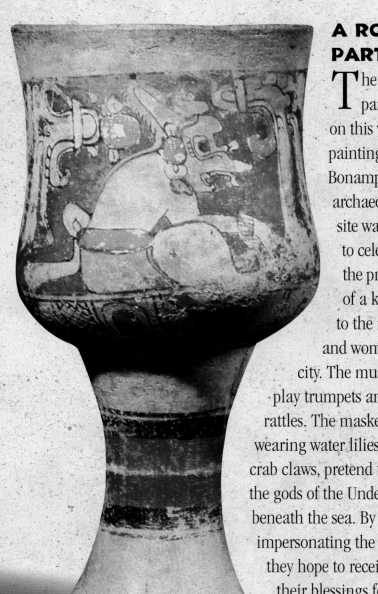

A ROYAL PARTY

The Maya party shown on this wall painting at the Bonampak archaeological site was held to celebrate the presentation of a king's son to the noble men and women of the city. The musicians play trumpets and shake rattles. The masked dancers, wearing water lilies and crab claws, pretend they are the gods of the Underworld beneath the sea. By impersonating the gods, they hope to receive their blessings for the young heir.

MEMBERS OF THE MAYA RULING CLASS DANCED IN PUBLIC DURING SACRED RITUALS. IN 1990 NIKOLAI GRUBE DECIPHERED THE GLYPH FOR "DANCE."

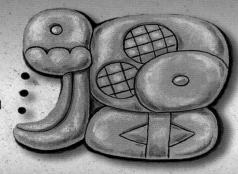

(Above left) This small clay drum was tucked under the drummer's left arm and played with his right hand. (Above right) A copy of the celebration scene at Bonampak.

HERE ARE SOME TIPS FOR HOLDING YOUR OWN MAYA PARTY.

FOOD: Serve make-your-own tortillas with salsa; guacamole and corn chips; refried beans; roast turkey; a guava and pineapple salad; sour sop ice cream; and a chocolate drink.

COSTUMES: Make fantastic masks using colorful feathers, glitter, and other art supplies. Or paint your faces like ancient Maya gods or royalty.

GAME: See page 45 for a Maya game.

WHAT HAPPENED TO THE ANCIENT MAYA?

Conquest of the sixteenth century.

When the Spaniards arrived, the Maya lived in villages, towns, and even some cities, much as they do today. But smallpox and other diseases brought by the Spaniards killed many of them. And for those who survived, the arrival of the Europeans changed their way of life forever. The last independent Maya kingdom fell in 1697.

In 1992, Rigoberta Menchu Tum, a K'iché Maya woman from Guatemala, won the Nobel Peace Prize in recognition of her work promoting peace and respect for the rights of indigenous peoples. She once said about the Maya: "We are not myths of the past, ruins in the jungle, or zoos. We are people and we want to be respected...." In fact, more than six million Maya live today in Guatemala, Belize, and Mexico. Many continue to grow maize, wear traditional dress, and practice some of the old sacred rituals as part of their Catholic faith. Although their ancient writing system is no longer used, the Maya still speak the beautiful languages of their ancestors.

Like her ancestors, this Maya woman weaves cloth on a backstrap loom.

Between A.D. 800 and 830, most of the Maya city states, including Calakmul and Tikal, suddenly collapsed. Some scholars think that crops may have stopped growing in the overused farmland surrounding the great cities. To escape starvation, people fled to other communities.

Although the Maya civilization was at its height during the golden era beginning in A.D. 250, it continued long after cities such as Tikal had been abandoned. In northern Yucatán in Mexico, the city of Chichén Itzá grew to a great size, and its architects built new styles of temples and palaces. Like the Aztec civilization, the Maya civilization was destroyed by the Spanish

SECRET CODES, GAMES, AND ACTIVITIES

SECRET NUMBER CODE

You and your friends can make your own secret code by using the Maya numbers to represent letters of the alphabet:

A = •; B = ••; C = •••

Or you can mix up the letters and numbers to make the code even more difficult to break:

A = ••••; B = ••; C = •

COUNTING HIGHER THAN TEN

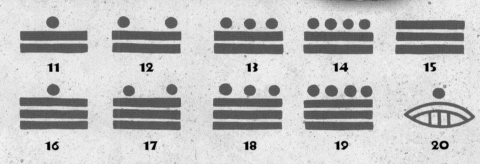

11   12   13   14   15

16   17   18   19   20

COUNTING HIGHER THAN TWENTY

Maya bar-and-dot numbers stretch down vertically by multiples of 20, rather than horizontally like our numbers. Here are three examples and one for you to solve:

Can you solve this

Answer on page 46

8000 (20 x 400)							
400 (20 x 20)				**400** (1 x 400)	•		
20 (1 x 20)	•	**40** (2 x 20)	••	**140** (7 x 20)	▬ ••		
0-19	◉	**15**	▬▬▬	**8**	▬ •••		
	20		**55**		**548**		**10,124**

RULER OF THE MAYA UNIVERSE – MAKE YOUR OWN STELA

On their stelae, the Maya wrote the ruler's name, political and religious titles, age, and family history, and important events in his or her life. Here's how you can make your own ruler of the universe stela using the GlyphMaster and the bar-and-dot numbers on pages 16 and 41. These are fun to do for friends and relatives on make-your-own birthday cards or on separate sheets of paper that can be framed. Be sure to translate your stela on the back of your card or piece of art. To make an interesting design, use different colored pencils and rub in different directions.

LORD

LADY

- Start by using the "lord" or "lady" glyph.
- Spell out your name (Mark is used as an example):

M   **A**   **R**   **K**

Maya experts make paper rubbings of stelae to study.

TIME LINE

EARLY PRECLASSIC (2000 B.C. TO 1000 B.C.)
Farming begins and villages grow up.

MIDDLE PRECLASSIC (1000 B.C. TO 400 B.C.)
600 B.C. — Tikal settled.
500 B.C. — First temples built.

LATE PRECLASSIC (400 B.C. TO A.D. 250)
100 B.C. — First writing appears.

CHILD OF (FATHER) **CHILD OF (MOTHER)**

● Add the "child of (father)" and "child of (mother)" glyphs.

● Spell out your father's first name and your mother's first name.

● Add your age (see page 16):

9

R   O   B   A   N   N   E

● Add the "count-of-friends" glyph with the number of friends beside it. If you want, you can add the names of your friends.

● If you want to include your pet, you can use the "parrot" for bird, "jaguar" for cat, and "bat" for other interesting animals you may own. If your family has more than one dog, cat, or bird, add the Maya number beside it.

HE OF 7 CAPTIVES **HE OR SHE OF 7 FRIENDS**

FISH **PARROT** **JAGUAR** **DOG** **BAT**

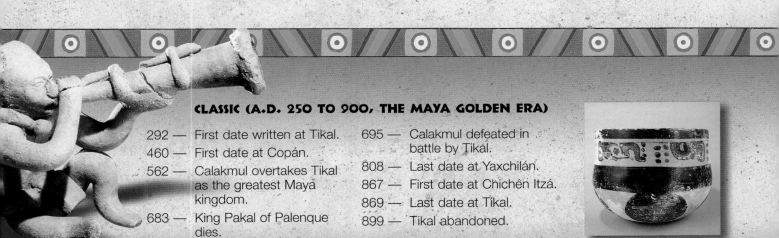

CLASSIC (A.D. 250 TO 900, THE MAYA GOLDEN ERA)

292 — First date written at Tikal.
460 — First date at Copán.
562 — Calakmul overtakes Tikal as the greatest Maya kingdom.
683 — King Pakal of Palenque dies.
695 — Calakmul defeated in battle by Tikal.
808 — Last date at Yaxchilán.
867 — First date at Chichén Itzá.
869 — Last date at Tikal.
899 — Tikal abandoned.

TAKE THE MAYA SYLLABARY CHALLENGE!

The glyphs standing for the letters from *a* to *z* in the GlyphMaster are how we've imagined what a Maya alphabet might look like — if the ancient Maya had used our writing system and spoken our language. We've made the GlyphMaster this way so that you can send quick secret messages. But the real Maya alphabet isn't an alphabet at all. It's called a "syllabary" and looks like the grid on the right.

The syllabary has glyphs that stand for a consonant followed by a vowel. There isn't a *d, f, g, j, q, r* or *v* because these sounds didn't exist in the Maya languages. The *ch', k', p', t'* and *tz'* are sounds that don't exist in our language. They're called glottal stops and are made by closing and opening the glottis, the opening between the vocal cords.

A conch shell trumpet.

To use the syllabary, you match up the letters (vowels) going down the page with the letters (consonants) across the top; for example *b* matched with *e* is 🔲. (We've used just one glyph for each letter combination in our syllabary, but codebreakers have found several different glyphs for some of the combinations and are still finding new ones.)

WRITING YOUR NAME

To write your name using the syllabary, first break your name into syllables; for example, Alyssa is A ly ssa. If your name contains sounds that weren't used by the Maya, choose ones that are close (*t* for *d*, *w* for *f*). Alyssa in Maya glyphs looks like this:

A　　　**LY**　　　**SSA**

POSTCLASSIC (A.D. 900 TO 1500)

1224 — Chichén Itzá abandoned.

1470 — K'iché Maya kingdom established in Guatemala.

COLONIAL

1502 — The Maya encounter the Spaniards for the first time when Christopher Columbus sails into the Gulf of Honduras.

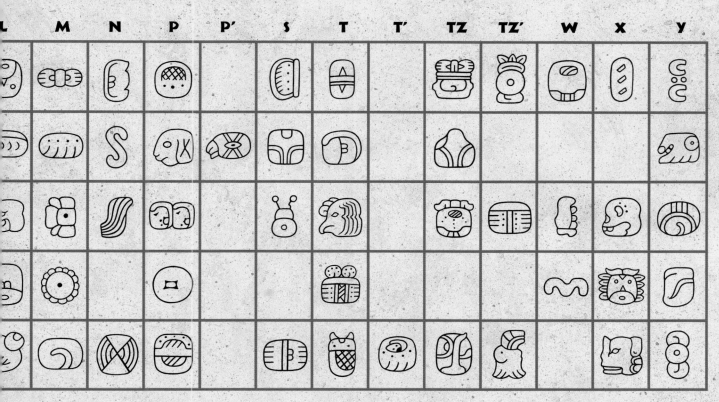

A MAGNIFICENT MAYA PARTY GAME

This game is based on a ritual dance. One dancer threw reeds and his partner caught them with a stick.

Partygoers form a large circle. Each one has a drum or pot, a whistle, or a rattle. The person on your right is your partner.

Each couple takes turns stepping into the middle of the circle. They stand about 3 feet (1 m) apart. One player is given ten plastic straws and holds them lengthwise in his or her hands. The other player holds his or her arms out with palms up.

At the count of three and with everyone in the circle beating drums, blowing whistles, and shaking rattles, the partner with the straws tosses them into his or her partner's arms. The partner quickly folds up his or her arms, catching as many straws as possible in the crooks of the elbows. The pair who catches the most straws after three turns wins.

A whistle in the shape of a musician.

1517 — Diseases brought by the Spaniards begin to infect and kill many Maya.

1524-1546 — Conquest of Maya by Spaniards.

1697 — Conquest of last independent Maya state (Tayasal).

1880 — Governments try to force the Maya to become laborers on plantations, destroying many cultural and agricultural traditions.

1952 — King Pakal's tomb discovered.

1992 — Rigoberta Menchu Tum wins the Nobel Peace Prize.

GREAT GLYPHMASTER IDEAS

SECRET MESSAGES

FAST CODES: Combine English words with a Maya glyph that stands for a word; for example, "Were you [glyph E] (surprised)?" Here are some fast code glyphs from the GlyphMaster. You and your friends can make up your own fast codes, too.

"Were you ?"

FAST CODE FOR FEELINGS: A = hungry; B = sick; E = surprised; I = shy; J = happy; L = angry; S = hurt.

FAST CODE FOR PLACES: In addition to the GlyphMaster glyphs for "house" and "bedroom," you could use two "book" glyphs for "library," the "scribe" sign under the "house" sign for "school," and the "K" sign under the "house" sign for "pool."

Library   *School*   *Pool*

PROJECTS TO MAKE WITH YOUR GLYPHMASTER

MAKE-YOUR-OWN MAYA BOOKPLATES See page 10.

MAKE-YOUR-OWN EMBLEM GLYPH See page 24. To make a Maya "do-not-disturb" sign for your bedroom door, first cut a hole the size of your doorknob at the top of a piece of paper. Rub your emblem glyph and the "Zotz, the bat" glyph below the hole on the sign.

GREETING CARD IDEAS See pages 24 and 42.

SUPER STELA

To make a super stela, add the following to the Ruler of the Maya Universe stela on page 42: the names of other members of your family; the "scribe/teacher" glyph followed by the name of your favorite writer or teacher; your favorite color (put the glyphs "red" and "white" together to make pink, "red" and "blue" together to make purple, etc.); anything else you want to add. On the opposite side of your stela, draw a picture of yourself so that it looks like a real stela.

SECRET NAME CODE
See page 27. (Remember, be careful whom you call a "vulture." No one wants to be known as an "excrement head"!)

SECRET NUMBER CODE
See page 41.

MASTER CODEBREAKER GAME

Test your code-breaking skills with a friend. Each of you makes up a message with the same number of glyphs. Then have a race to see who can break the other's message first.

SOLUTION TO MAYA MATH PROBLEM FROM PAGE 41

8000 (1 x 8,000)	●
2,000 (5 x 400)	▬
120 (6 x 20)	● ▬
4 (4 x 1)	● ● ● ●
10,124	

GLOSSARY

archaeologist: a person trained to excavate the buried remains of ancient cultures. They study the objects, buildings, and writing of these cultures to discover more about the lives and customs of people of the past.

Aztecs: a Nahuatl-speaking people whose empire in Mexico was conquered by the Spanish in 1519.

code: the rules and symbols of a writing system.

codex (plural "codices"): an accordion-folded book made of paper.

consonant: sounds that are formed by stopping the air flow from the mouth, such as *b, c, d, f, g*.

decipher: to translate the signs of a language or writing system.

ear flare: the part of an ear ornament that rests directly on the ear lobe and flares outward, forming a circle or square that covers a large part of the ear (see page 37). A string with jade beads, or a small bar, is put through a pierced hole in the ear lobe to hold the flare in place.

epigrapher: a person who studies systems of writing.

hieroglyph (short form "glyph"): in Maya writing, a sign that stands for a word, syllable, or vowel.

indigenous peoples: a group of people who are known to be the earliest people ever to have lived in an area.

Mesoamericans: people from southern Mexico, Guatemala, Belize, and western El Salvador and Honduras who lived in these areas prior to the arrival of Christopher Columbus.

sarcophagus: a stone coffin.

scribe: a person who wrote books by hand before modern printing methods were invented.

stela (plural "stelae"): in the Maya region, an upright stone monument on which a ruler's image and family history are recorded.

syllabary: a grid of signs that is a guide to the pronunciation or interpretation of syllables.

syllable: a vowel-consonant combination, or a vowel alone, that represents a sound or the building block of a word.

tribute: payment, usually in goods such as textiles or food, owed by one person to another, or paid by one village, town, or city to another.

vowel: sounds made by the free flow of air from the mouth, such as *a, e, i, o, u*.

SELECTED BIBLIOGRAPHY

The Ancient Maya by Robert J. Sharer (Stanford University Press, 1994)

The Art of the Maya Scribe by Michael D. Coe and Justin Kerr (Thames and Hudson, 1997)

Breaking the Maya Code by Michael D. Coe (Thames and Hudson, 1992)

The Code of Kings by Linda Schele and Peter Mathews (Scribner, 1998)

A Forest of Kings by Linda Schele and David Freidel (William Morrow, 1990)

Incidents of Travel in Central America, Chiapas and Yucatán by John Stephens (Murray, 1841)

The Maya: Life, Myth and Art by Timothy Laughton (Duncan Baird Publishers, 1998)

Maya Explorer by Victor Wolfgang von Hagen (Chronicle Books, 1975)

Notebook for the XXIVth Maya Hieroglyphic Forum at Texas (The University of Texas at Austin, 2000)

Painting the Maya Universe by Dorie Reents-Budet (Duke University Press, 1994)

PICTURE CREDITS

INDEX

almanacs, 19
architecture, 8
arithmetic, 9, 17, 41
arithmetic, Roman, 17
astronomy, 19
Aztec civilization, 10, 17, 34, 40

ball court glyph, 34
ball games, 34-35
balls, rubber, 9, 34-35
Belize, 40
Berlin, Heinrich, 24
birthdate, your Maya, 21
bloodletting rituals, 33, 37
body piercing, 37
Bonampak, 37, 38
books, 10, 12
burial of ruler, 26, 33

cacao, 17, 36
Calakmul, 25, 40, 43
calendars, 9, 19, 20-21, 22, 23, 30
captives, 19, 32, 37
Catherwood, Frederick, 4-7, 22
ceiba tree, 17, 37
Champollion, Jean François, 12
chewing gum, 24
Chichén Itzá, 7, 19, 34, 40
chicle, 24
chocolate, 17, 36
Cholan language, 27-28
cities, 4-7, 8-9, 40
clothing, 37
Coba, 32
codex, 12, 13
Coe, Michael, 26-27, 28
Columbus, Christopher, 44
Copán, 4, 31, 34, 43
corn, 16, 40
creation story, 14

dancing, 38
de Bourbourg, Abbé Charles
    Brasseur, 14
de Landa, Diego, 10, 12, 17
death, 14, 17, 30, 33
Dresden Codex, 12, 13, 17

ear flares, 36, 37
ear piercing, 37
Egyptian hieroglyphs, 12, 24
epigraphers, 7

face painting, 37, 39
farming, 16, 40
feathers, 16
foreheads, flattened, 37
Förstemann, Ernst, 17, 19

games and activities, 41-46
glottal stops, 44
GlyphMaster activities, 10, 24, 27,
    41-43, 46
glyphs
    calendar, 20
    date, 30
    different meanings for
        same, 30
    emblem, 24-25, 30
    event, 30
    family, 31, 43
    individual styles, 31
    introductory, 23
    name and title, 30
    name-tagging, 36
    space fillers between, 18
gods, 14, 17, 33, 37, 38
golden era, 8, 25, 37, 40, 43
Grube, Nikolai, 38
Guatemala, 14, 33, 40

Hero Twins, 14, 35
hieroglyphs, Egyptian, 12, 24
hieroglyphs, Maya. See glyphs
Huanahpu, 14
huipil (blouse), 37
Hunter, Annie, 22

inventions, 9

jaguar, 29
jewelry, 36, 37

Kelley, David, 27, 28
K'iche Maya kingdom, 44
kings, 8, 19, 25, 30, 33, 37, 38
Knorosov, Yuri, 27, 28

Lhuillier, Alberto Ruz, 26
logographs, 29
Lounsbury, Floyd, 27

maize, 16, 40
Mathews, Peter, 26-27, 28, 36
Maudslay, Alfred Percival, 22, 23
Menchu Tum, Rigoberta, 40
Mexico, 10, 17, 40
Middleworld, 17
missionaries, 10
money, 17

name-tagging, 36
numbers, 17, 41

offerings to gods, 33
Overworld, 17, 33

Pakal, 26, 28, 43, 45
Palenque, 25, 26-28
parties, 38-39
Piedras Negras, 24, 25
Popol Vuh, 14, 35
Proskouriakoff, Tatiana, 24, 25

queens, 33, 37

religious rituals, 20, 33, 35

sacrifice, 26, 33
sapodilla tree, 24
Schele, Linda, 26-27, 28
Seibal, 24
Spanish Conquest, 7, 8, 10, 40, 44
star wars, 18, 19
stela, 4, 42
Stephens, John Lloyd, 4-7, 22
Stuart, David, 32-33
Stuart, George, 32, 33
syllabary, 29, 44-45

tattooing, 37
teeth, decoration of, 37
Tekun Uman, 10
Temple of the Inscriptions
    (Palenque), 26
Tikal, 25, 40, 42, 43
time line, 42-45

Underworld, 14, 17

Venus, 19

wars, 10, 19
weapons, 10, 19
World Tree, 17, 37

Xbalanque, 14
Xibalba, 14, 17

Yax Pasah, 31
Yaxchilán, 24, 43
Yucatán Peninsula, 6, 7, 24
Yucatec language, 27, 28

zero, 9, 17
Zotz, 14

ACKNOWLEDGMENTS

I would like to thank Elizabeth Graham, Simon Martin, and Dorie Reents-Budet for their expert advice and Sarah Jane English for her wonderful illustrations. Michael Coe's book, *Breaking the Maya Code*, was particularly helpful. Many thanks as well to Nan Froman, Gord Sibley, Dale Vokey, David Pendergast, Justin and Barbara Kerr, David Greene, Lindsey Magee, Mara Fraccaro, and Alba Agosto. At Madison Press Books, Hugh Brewster, Susan Barrable, Wanda Nowakowska, Sandra Hall, Mireille Majoor, and Susan Aihoshi deserve a special thank you for their help and patience.

Text, illustrations, design, and compilation © 2001 The Madison Press Limited

First published in Canada by
Scholastic Canada Ltd.
175 Hillmount Road
Markham, Ontario L6C 1Z7

Canadian Cataloguing in Publication Data

Coulter, Laurie, 1951-
   Secrets in stone: all about Maya hieroglyphs

"A Scholastic/Madison Press book"
Includes index.
ISBN 0-439-98790-3 (bound)
ISBN 0-439-98791-1 (pbk.)

1. Mayan languages — Writing — Juvenile literature. I. English, Sarah Jane 1956-.
II. Title.
F1435.3.W75C68 2000   j497'.415211
C00-932742-8

10 9 8 7 6 5 4 3 2 1

Editorial Director:
   Hugh M. Brewster

Editor:
   Nan Froman

Editorial Assistance:
   Susan Aihoshi, Ingrid Mida

Book Design:
   Gordon Sibley Design Inc.

Production Director:
   Susan Barrable

Production Manager:
   Sandra L. Hall

Color Separation:
   Colour Technologies

Printing and Binding:
   EuroGrafica S.p.A., Vicenza

Secrets in Stone was produced by Madison Press Books, which is under the direction of Albert E. Cummings.

Produced by
Madison Press Books
1000 Yonge Street
Toronto, Ontario
Canada M4W 2K2
Printed and bound in Italy